DATE DUE

AP 2 '98		
DEC 3 '03		

DEMCO 38-296

P9-AGG-689

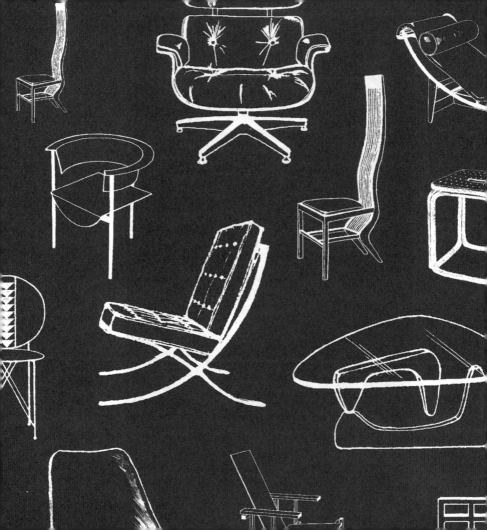

ABC
of design

by Lynn Gordon

Illustrations by D/M Joy

CHRONICLE BOOKS
SAN FRANCISCO

Copyright © 1996 by Lynn Gordon. No part of this book may be repro-
duced in any form without written permission from the publisher.

Library of Congress Cataloging-in-Publication Data available
ISBN 0-8118-1141-7

Concept and Design: Lynn Gordon
Illustration and Graphic Design: North American Stijl Life
Jacket Design: North American Stijl Life

Printed in Hong Kong

Distributed in Canada by
Raincoast Books
8680 Cambie Street
Vancouver, B.C. V6P 6M9

10 9 8 7 6 5 4 3 2 1

Chronicle Books
275 Fifth Street
San Francisco, CA 94103

For my father, who taught me at age seven the difference between Italian and French chair legs and who infused his lessons with a memorable wit.

And for Amelia & Karrie, who continue to try to make sense of design.

Introduction

Sometimes a chair is just a chair. Sometimes a chair is your cat's kingdom. That can be a problem. And sometimes, a chair is a letter in the alphabet. Ah, you say, that's absurd. But it's true. You will see it too. A bit of design history, when lined up arm-to-arm, leg-to-leg, makes complete alphabetical sense. Maybe now you'll look upon these design classics more skeptically. And from your sideways glance you'll see something new—maybe the solution to a mathematical proof, maybe the missing ingredient to the family's goulash recipe. It's as simple as A through Z. Perhaps this is all too "tongue-in-chic" for you. Perhaps you had better sit down. And stare. At a chair. What do you see?

Contents

Alvar Aalto The Finnish architect-designer Alvar Aalto (1898–1976) believed that "the human imagination must have free room in which to unfold." Both his buildings and his furniture embody this freedom. His natural Scandinavian wood furniture was designed to complement the airy warmth of his buildings. Aalto rejected the cold tubular steel of modern furniture in favor of Finnish birchwood, which he bent and laminated (in a process he patented in 1933) to take on more curvaceous form. His company, Artek—which he founded with his wife and collaborator, Aino Marsio—continues to produce his designs. Aalto defined his chairs as "multidimensional, sculpturelike wooden forms." The curves of his 1946 Cantilevered Armchair are as graceful as the chair is comfortable.

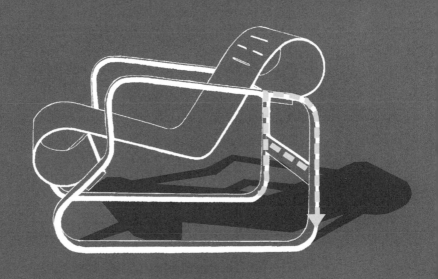

Marcel Breuer At 23, Marcel Breuer (1902–1981) designed the first chair made of tubular steel, a portent of modern furniture design. Designed for abstract painter Wassily Kandinsky, the Wassily Chair was immediately recognized as a design classic. Breuer left his home in Hungary to study painting in Vienna, but he later abandoned the academy for the Bauhaus. Inspired by the school's aesthetic blend of expressionism and functionalism, Breuer became the master of the Bauhaus carpentry workshop. His fascination with standardization and mass production as modern manufacturing for a modern age reflected his design philosophy: "to find the simplest way." His 1928 Cesca Chair (named after his daughter), made of bent tubular steel with a comfortable caned seat and back, is still one of the most widely used chairs today.

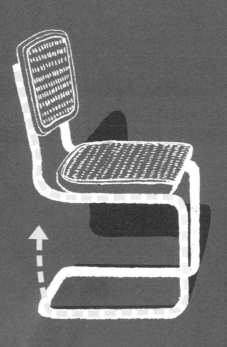

Le Corbusier

The Swiss painter, designer, architect, and urban planner Le Corbusier (born Charles Edouard Jeanneret, 1887–1965) became a leader of the modern movement in architecture and design. Renowned for the idea that "a house is a machine for living in," Corbusier envisioned furniture as universal "domestic equipment," which should be scaled to the proportions of the human body. The point of his "machine aesthetic," however, was not that design should become machinelike, but that mass production and functional design could create less expensive and better furniture—a reaction against the notion that "good" furniture was a privilege of the upper classes alone. Designed with Charlotte Perriand, his Chaise Longue of tubular steel and black leather, dubbed "a rest machine" by Le Corbusier, is easily adjustable for maximum comfort.

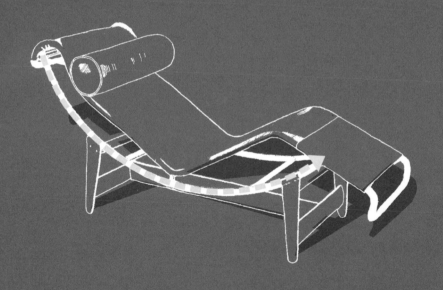

Andre Dubreuil Frenchman

Andre Dubreuil (b. 1951) began his career as a trompe l'oeil muralist and antiques dealer in London. When a friend taught him to weld, Dubreuil discovered a buried talent and quickly adopted wrought iron as his medium, replacing his paintbrush with the blowtorch. Together with friends Tom Dixon and Mark Brazier-Jones, Dubreuil became a leader of Great Britain's art furniture movement in the 1980s. Dubreuil eschews sketches and tape measures, preferring to work spontaneously from an idea. His furniture is designed for the collector and so, unlike the leaders of modernism, Dubreuil does not design for mass production. Although Dubreuil originally produced a limited number each month, his Spine Chair (1987) became so popular he finally agreed to allow an Italian company to manufacture it.

Charles Eames American

Charles Eames (1907–1978) is widely considered one of the creative geniuses of the twentieth century. He was first recognized in 1940 when he won, along with Eero Saarinen, the New York Museum of Modern Art's "Organic Design in Home Furnishing" competition. With his lifetime collaborator and wife, Ray, Eames explored the philosophy of creating every piece with its own integrity and "in its own time and space." Their projects ranged from furniture and architecture to experimental films. Although Charles and Ray worked hard on the development of shapely molded plywood chairs, Eames's 1956 Lounge Chair and Ottoman of leather and rosewood was the first chair he designed with both physical and psychological comfort in mind.

Jean-Michel Frank French designer Jean-Michel Frank's (1895–1941) interior design was so spare that, upon viewing one of his rooms, writer and artist Jean Cocteau quipped, "pity the burglars got everything." Frank wanted to distill furniture to its essence, believing that simple forms become exquisite through the use of surprising materials and exacting detail. Before his suicide, Frank had befriended many of Paris' cultural elite, including Diaghilev, Picasso, Stravinsky, and Chanel. The great uncle of diarist Anne Frank, he is said to have dashed off the design for the Parsons Table (1920s) as a way to teach perspective drawing to his students at the Parsons School of Design in Paris.

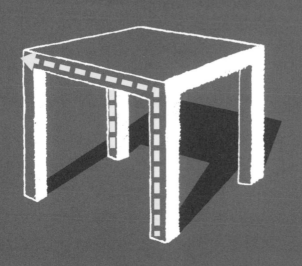

Eileen Gray The Irish-born interior designer and architect Eileen Gray (1879–1976) successfully combined the exoticism of early Art Deco with the modernist trends of the 1930s. Gray's work was highly original, combining unusual forms, materials, and finishes (particularly the use of oriental lacquer, which she studied with Sugawara, the Japanese master of this medium). In her first significant design commission, a home for a Parisian model, Gray established her signature look by dividing the space with lacquered screens and draping zebra and leopard skins across tubular furniture. Bauhaus-founder Walter Gropius's enthusiasm for her work facilitated her movement into designing apartment buildings and houses. Her side table (1927), with a smoked-glass top and adjustable height, reflects her elegant yet practical style.

Josef Hoffmann Austrian designer Josef Hoffmann (1870–1956) believed that "a house must be created as a perfect whole." This concept developed through his association with the Vienna Secession movement—a group of young artists and intellectuals who proclaimed their break with the past. In 1903 Hoffmann cofounded the *Wiener Werkstatte* (Vienna Workshop) with artist Gustav Klimt as a collaboration of artists and craftsmen. The Workshop produced furniture, metalwork and leatherwork for more than thirty years. Hoffmann designed not only buildings and furniture but also other domestic objects and surfaces such as tableware, textiles, and even wallpaper. Inspired by the work of Charles Mackintosh, Hoffmann's Armloffel Chair (1908) reflects his integration of smooth surfaces with geometrical detail.

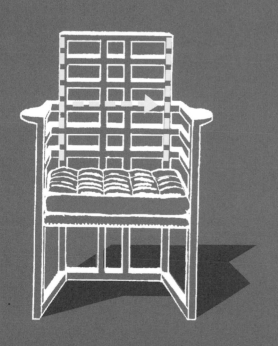

Arata Isozaki "Architecture is a machine for the production of meaning," says Japanese architect Arata Isozaki (b. 1931). For Isozaki, meaning often includes a sense of irony and wit, as evidenced in the furniture he designed for the Memphis collection in Italy. In partnership with his teacher Kenzo Tange, founder of the Metabolist movement, Isozaki became the chief architect of the 1970 Japan World Exposition in Osaka. His book *The Dismantling of Architecture* is a manifesto of the principles he applied to such projects as the Museum of Contemporary Art in Los Angeles and the Palladium Disco in New York City. The back of the Monroe Chair (1973) waves whimsically at passersby.

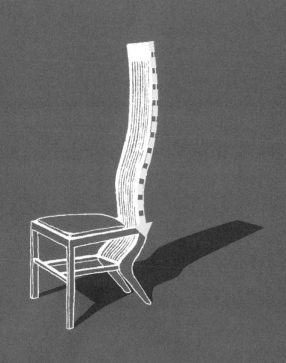

Arne Jacobsen Although Danish architect Arne Jacobsen (1902–1971) originally apprenticed as a bricklayer, his hands-on interest in diverse materials led him to the design of furniture in fiberglass, chromed steel, cast aluminum, foam padding, vinyl, leather, plywood, and molded latex. Bringing the new religion of modernism to Denmark, Jacobsen blended the efficiency of industry with the artist's imagination and the craftsman's attention to detail. Jacobsen's design work ranged from international hotels and massive public buildings to salt and pepper shakers and other objects for the home. His internationally lauded Ant Chair (1955), created from nine layers of wood—steamed, molded, and glued— was the first Danish chair designed for mass production, and it is still in production today.

Florence & Hans Knoll

Florence and Hans Knoll's professional partnership developed through their mutual admiration of the artist/craftsperson ideal developed at the Bauhaus. A German cabinetmaker from a furniture-making family, Hans Knoll (1914–1955) founded a furniture company in 1943 that later became Knoll International. With his American wife, architect Florence Schust (b. 1917), Knoll manufactured the revolutionary furniture of the day: Mies van der Rohe's Barcelona Chair, Harry Bertoia's Wire Basket Chair, and Eero Saarinen's Womb Chair among many others. None of the designs they manufactured have been as widely copied as the Butterfly Chair—designed by Jorge Ferrari-Hardoy, Juan Kurchan, and Antonio Bonet in 1938. First manufactured by Knoll, over five million copies of the Butterfly Chair have been produced.

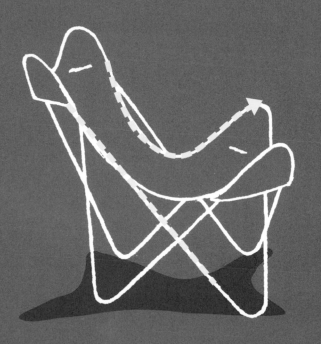

Wassili & Hans Luckhardt

"Steel furniture is a living expression of our striving for rhythm, functionality, hygiene, cleanliness, lightness, simplicity of form," wrote German architect Hans Luckhardt (1890–1954) in 1930. Hans and his brother Wassili (1889–1972) began their careers in Berlin in the early 1920s when the dearth of paying clients meant their utopian, expressionistic designs would never be built. In the 1940s their most accomplished work wasn't realized because it was in conflict with Hitler's political and aesthetic agendas. They did build experimental housing and create bent metal-plated furniture during this period. The Luckhardts' tubular steel chair, Model S36 (1930), embodies Hans's statement that "a well-formed piece of steel furniture possesses an exclusive, independent aesthetic value of its own."

Charles Rennie Mackintosh

Scotsman Charles Rennie Mackintosh (1868–1928) blended the craft emphasis, later celebrated by the Bauhaus, with art nouveau. His design output was small, but his influence was far reaching. He designed buildings, interiors, textiles, stained class, and posters. In 1920 he retired to France to pursue watercolor painting and died in relative obscurity. His designs were rediscovered in the 1930s and hailed as thoroughly modern. His high backed chairs, built of darkly stained oak, inspired Josef Hoffmann. Mackintosh designed each chair for a specific setting. The supervisor of Miss Cranston's Willow Tea Rooms was to sit in the Willow I Curved Lattice-Back Chair (1904) and relay the waiters' orders to the kitchen crew.

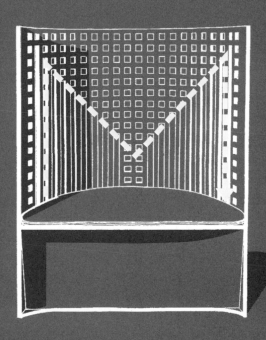

Isamu Noguchi American-born sculptor Isamu Noguchi (1904–1988) grew up in Japan and Indiana. As a young man, he made portrait busts and served as assistant to sculptor Constantin Brancusi in Paris. His wide breadth of sculptural projects range from radios for Zenith to sculpture gardens such as the one he designed for the Bienecke Rare Book Library at Yale University. Approaching all his work with a sculptural sensibility, Noguchi has developed a distinctive aesthetic throughout his varied projects. For over forty years he designed the stage sets for modern dance legend Martha Graham while also working as a product and furniture designer. His sensuously sculptural In50 Table (1944), a rounded plate glass triangle floating on a free-form wooden base, is still in production.

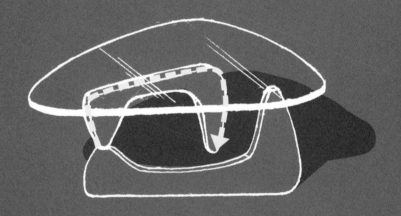

Otto Wagner Austrian Otto Wagner (1841–1918) believed modern life at the turn of the century demanded fresh design. "We do not walk around in the costumes of Louis XIV," he sniffed, dismissing the nineteenth-century trend towards stylistic revivals. His book *Moderne Architektur* (1895) became the theoretical cornerstone of the modernist movement. As architectural professor at the Vienna Academy of Art, Wagner planted the seeds of his modernist principles with a new generation of architects (including Peter Behrens). Wagner designed the Vienna Postal Savings Bank as well as the functional furniture inside. The amount of metal used in each chair or stool signaled the sitter's status in the bank hierarchy. Wagner's Postal Savings Bank Stool (1906) conveniently includes a cutout handhold in the perforated seat.

Gio Ponti Italy's preeminent twentieth-century designer, Gio Ponti (1891–1979) began his career making boldly painted urns, vases, and goblets as well as elegant cutlery. In 1928, he began publishing what has become the seminal architecture and design magazine *Domus*, which he continued to edit until his death 51 years later. A versatile designer, he built churches and office buildings, but also designed cars, toilets, and sewing machines. Deeply rooted in his Italian culture, Ponti's work includes an expresso machine and settings and costumes for Milan's opera, La Scala. He also helped found the Italian Movement of Rational Architecture. His lightweight wood Super-leggera Chair 699 (1957) was inspired by a classic Italian fishing chair.

Queen Anne Style Under the reign of Queen Anne (1702–14) a new English national style of furniture developed that rejected ornate carving and design in favor of simple beauty and comfort derived from the use of repeating curves. The two significant characteristics of this style were the curvaceous yet unadorned cabriole leg, which became the standard for furniture leg design for about half a century, and the use of walnut veneering in place of elaborately carved surface designs. The simple and dignified Queen Anne style persisted for a decade after the Queen's death, until around 1725. Considered "the most pleasing of all English chairs," the popular Queen Anne splat-back chair demonstrates a simple beauty through the coordination of curved lines in the cabriole legs, hoop back, and vase-shaped splats, which also created a new standard of comfort for its time.

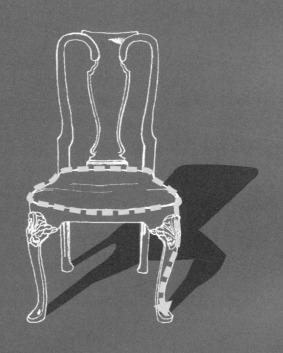

Gerrit Rietveld

Dutch designer Gerrit Rietveld (1888–1964), a carpenter's son who studied architecture at night school, embraced the ideas developed by Theo van Doesburg and others in the journal *De Stijl*. Taking to heart the idea that "the aim of design is to define space," Rietveld insisted that the purpose of a chair is not comfort, but rather "to make space tangible . . . awareness is more important than ease." Rietveld, like the other adherents to the principles of Neo-Plasticism, investigated geometric abstraction in all of his work—lines were strictly vertical or horizontal; color was essential to design and never applied merely as embellishment. Rietveld's internationally famous Red-Blue Chair (1918) embodies these ideas. Against a black wall, the chair's black frame fades away and the colorful rectangular planes of seat and back define the chair in space.

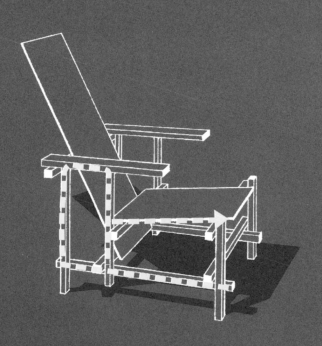

Eero Saarinen The son of a sculptor and world-renowned architect Eliel Saarinen, Finnish-born architect Eero Saarinen (1910–1961) won first prize in a matchstick design contest when he was twelve. During his study at Yale in the 1920s, Eero absorbed the most modern European trends, as well as the ideas of his teacher, color theorist Josef Albers. The effect of this education is embodied in his declaration of the three fundamental principles of modern design: "function, structure, and being part of our time." Working out of Michigan, he designed the TWA Terminal at New York's Kennedy Airport as a huge bird to evoke "the drama and specialness and excitement of travel." Saarinen developed the Pedestal Chairs (1956) with his pedestal table in an effort to "clear out the slum of legs. I wanted to make the air all one thing again."

Michael Thonet

Prussian cabinetmaker Michael Thonet (1796–1871) melded the efficiency of the machine with the beauty of craft when he invented the bentwood process in 1840. By taking a thin strip of flexible steel, clamping it to a piece of steamed wood and shaping that wood into graceful curves, Thonet created a family of furnishings that included chairs, tables, and a chaise lounge. In 1853, Thonet turned his business over to his five sons, who were able to realize the potential of this revolutionary manufacturing process by taking their father's invention into mass production. Michael Thonet's Vienna Chair (1859), durable and easy to assemble, is not only still in production but is the greatest selling chair of all time.

Shigeru Uchida Best known as one of Japan's most celebrated interior designers, Shigeru Uchida (b. 1945) has also made significant contributions to architecture and furniture design. His belief that "a single designer should be able to work on several levels in several domains" is the cornerstone philosophy to Studio 80, the multifaceted design firm he cofounded in 1981 with two other leading designers, including his wife, Ikuyo Mitsuhashi. Issey Miyake and Hanae Mori have utilized Uchida's furniture and interior design to complement their own clothing design. Although he credits Italian modernism as a significant early influence, his work is most distinctive in its adherence to traditional Japanese principles of elegance and restraint. Part of Studio 80's own line of furniture, this untitled chair of 1988 reflects his minimalistic approach.

Henry-Clement van de Velde

"Ugliness corrupts not only the eyes, but the heart and mind," declared Flemish painter and architect Henry-Clement van de Velde (1863–1957). His work bridged two centuries and evolved from a geometric art nouveau wholism toward more modern and process-driven thinking. His early rooms featured art nouveau touches on windows, carpets, and walls. He even designed dresses to highlight these interiors and was said to have advised his wife on which food to serve to enhance his designs. His furniture was the plain and calming element among the multilayered decorative touches in his interiors. Van de Velde led the Weimar School of Arts and Crafts until Walter Gropius took over in 1919 and rechristened the school the Bauhaus. Van de Velde designed this chair (1895) to go in a home he also designed for himself.

Frank Lloyd Wright

Probably the most famous name in American architecture, Frank Lloyd Wright (1867–1959) designed thoroughly modern public buildings, comfortable homes, and furniture (which he believed was a crucial part of the total environment). Wright's work grew out of the arts and crafts movement, but was also later influenced by the functionalism of the 1920s and 30s. His buildings, such as the house he called *Fallingwater* (near Pittsburgh) and the Solomon R. Guggenheim Museum in New York, are landmark American designs. John Wright, his son, claims that Wright created the first piece of modern American furniture. Wright himself claims that the office furniture he designed for the Larkin Administration Building in 1904 was the first metal office furniture ever. The bright red Midway Chair (1914), which he designed for a beer garden, was a casualty of the Prohibition era.

X-Based Furniture (Ludwig Mies van der Rohe) Every design of German architect and designer Ludwig Mies van der Rohe (1886–1969) embodies his philosophy that "less is more." The son of a stone mason in the medieval city of Aachen, Mies van der Rohe became known for his sensitivity to materials and meticulous detailing, which can be seen in every level of his work from furniture design and exposition architecture to his shimmering glass skyscrapers. Appointed director of the Bauhaus in the 1930s, he eventually shut down the school to protest the Nazi movement and fled to the United States. Although he was an exemplar of modern principles in design, Mies van der Rohe's creations did not always start from an immersion in the processes of mass production. The sleekly modern appearance of his luxurious and costly Barcelona Chair and Ottoman (1929) belies the laborious handwork necessary to produce it.

Sori Yanagi Japanese interior designer Sori Yanagi (b. 1915) was taught by his philospher father that "what is useful is beautiful." Although he specializes in fashion boutiques and other retail shops, Yanagi resolutely resists commercialism, and he expresses this resistance in his belief that "true design consists in challenging the prevailing fashion." With his father he wrote *Mingei: Masterpieces of Japanese Folkcraft*, a book on traditional Japanese design. He has designed not only wooden furniture, but also ceramic pieces, a sales kiosk, and a sound wall for a Japanese superhighway. Yanagi finds the fundamental facts of human life within the purity of his many diverse designs, from porcelain vessels and lacquer bowls to iron kettles and rich kimonos. Yanagi's Butterfly Stool (1954), composed of plywood and steel, embodies the simplicity and elegance of the Japanese aesthetic.

Zaha Hadid While not very interested in technology per se, Bagdad-born architect Zaha Hadid (b. 1950) draws inspiration from its effects, and her work embodies the fragmentation and acceleration that has characterized the technology-friendly culture of this century. Hadid studied mathematics at the American University of Beirut before moving to London. In 1983, she gained international attention with her winning design for "The Peak," a prestigious competition to design an exclusive Hong Kong club. Working with a team of designers, painters, architects, and engineers, Hadid creates buildings which she envisions as animated extensions of human life—abstract and sculptural forms in which function plays only a secondary role. These sculptural forms are evident in her Projection in Red Sofa (1987), where colorful forms float through space.

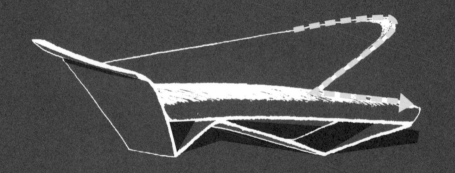

Sources

Banger, Albrecht, and Karl Michael Armer. *80s Style Designs of the Decade*. New York: Abbeville, 1990.

Benevolo, Leonardo. *History of Modern Architecture, Vol. 2*. Cambridge: MIT Press, 1978.

Blaser, Werner. *Mies van der Rohe Furniture and Interiors*. New York: Barrons, 1982.

Boger, Louise Ade. *Furniture Past & Present*. New York: Doubleday, 1966.

Byars, Mel. *The Design Encyclopedia*. New York: John Wiley & Sons, 1994.

Capella, Juli, and Quim Larrea. *Designed by Architects in the 1980s*. New York: Rizzoli, 1987.

Dormer, Peter. *Design Since 1945*. London: Thames and Hudson, 1993.

Emery, Marc. *Furniture by Architects*. New York: Harry N. Abrams, 1983.

Gandy, Charles. *Contemporary Classsics: Furniture of the Masters*. New York: McGraw-Hill, 1981.

Garner, Philippe. *Twentieth-Century Furniture*. New York: Van Nostrand Reinhold, 1980.

———. *Contemporary Decorative Arts from 1940 to the Present*. New York: Facts on File, 1980.

Jervis, Simon. *The Penguin Dictionary of Design and Designers*. New York: Penguin Books, 1984.

Kalir, Jane. *Viennese Design and the Weiner Werkstatte*. New York: Galerie St. Eteinne/George Braziller, 1986.

MacLean, Charles. "Forging Ahead." *House & Garden*, November 1989, 150–57.

Meadmore, Clement. *The Modern Chair*. New York: Van Nostrand Reinhold, 1975.

McQuiston, Liz. *Women in Design*. New York: Rizzoli, 1988.

Morgan, Ann Lee. *Contemporary Designers*. New York: MacMillan, 1984.

Russell, Frank, and Philippe Garner. *A Century of Chair Design*. New York: Rizzoli, 1980.

Sparke, Penny. *Modern Japanese Furniture*. New York: E. P. Dutton, 1987.

———. *An Introduction to Design & Culture in the Twentieth Century*. New York: Harper & Row, 1987.

———. *Furniture: Twentieth-Century Design*. London: Bell & Hyman, 1986.

Stimpson, Miriam. *Modern Furniture Classics*. New York: Whitney Library of Design, 1987.

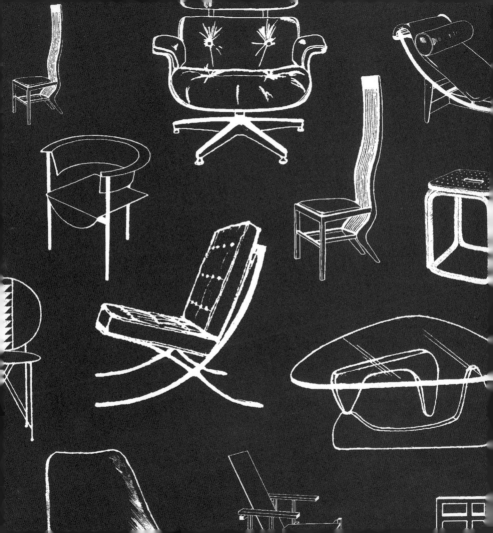